T0394796

BEHIND THE BRAND

DUNGEONS & DRAGONS

BY JOY LAO-SE

BELLWETHER MEDIA • MINNEAPOLIS, MN

Blastoff! Discovery launches a new mission: reading to learn. Filled with facts and features, each book offers you an exciting new world to explore!

BLASTOFF! UNIVERSE

BLASTOFF! Beginners — GRADE K

BLASTOFF! READERS — GRADES 1-3

DISCOVERY — GRADE 4

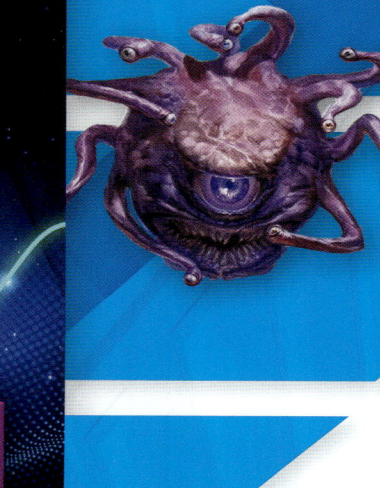

This edition first published in 2025 by Bellwether Media, Inc.

Library of Congress Cataloging-in-Publication Data

LC record for Dungeons & Dragons available at:
https://lccn.loc.gov/2024046804

Editor: Betsy Rathburn   Series Designer: Andrea Schneider   Book Designer: Josh Brink

Printed in the United States of America, North Mankato, MN.

TABLE OF
CONTENTS

SETTING THE SCENE

A group of friends gathers to play Dungeons & Dragons. Their **campaign** begins around a campfire. The sun has set and the entire party is settling in. An Elven wizard flips through her spellbook. Beside her, a Dwarf fighter sharpens his sword.

The quiet evening is interrupted by the sound of howling wolves. One of the party members rolls a nature check to learn more about the wolves. They roll a 17! This score is high enough to learn that the wolves are hungry. The party gets ready to fight!

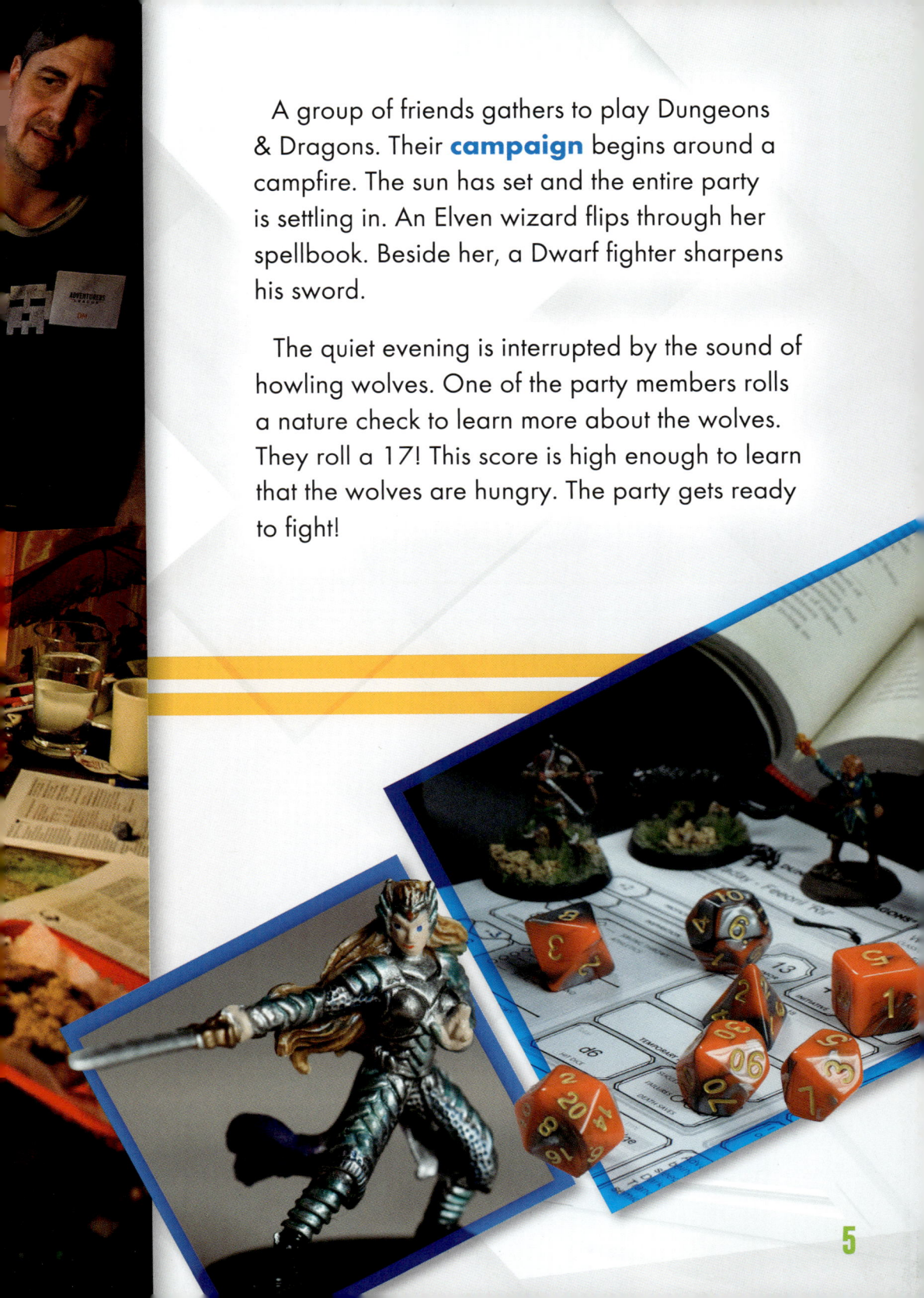

BUILDING A NEW WORLD

WOTC HEADQUARTERS
RENTON, WASHINGTON

Dungeons & Dragons (D&D) is a tabletop **role-playing game**. Players love its creative storytelling and open-ended play style. The game is owned by a company called Wizards of the Coast (WotC). WotC has **headquarters** in Renton, Washington.

To play the game, a **dungeon master** (DM) leads players on a campaign through a fantasy world. Players fight enemies, explore new areas, and collect items. Along the way, they gain experience points and level up their characters. Maps and figurines help players keep track of the game. Some use **apps** to play more easily.

WIZARDS OF THE COAST HEADQUARTERS

RENTON, WASHINGTON

DAVE ARNESON

20-SIDED DICE

D&D was created by Gary Gygax and Dave Arneson. When he was young, Gary enjoyed playing **wargames**. Players used different **strategies** to win in wars. Gary wanted to improve the games. He created a new version that used 20-sided dice. This made dice rolls more random.

In 1971, Gary created a new game called *Chainmail*. It took place during **medieval** times. Extra rules let players use magic! Many people liked the new game. Gary sold around 100 copies each month.

CHAINMAIL

Soon, Gary began working with Dave Arneson. Together, they created Dungeons & Dragons. It was based on *Chainmail*. In 1974, Gary released D&D through his company, Tactical Studies Rules (TSR). In less than a year, D&D sold 1,000 copies!

GARY GYGAX

BORN July 27, 1938, in Chicago, Illinois

DIED March 4, 2008

ROLE Co-creator of D&D and leader of Tactical Studies Rules

ACCOMPLISHMENTS

Grew D&D to be the most popular tabletop role-playing game in the world

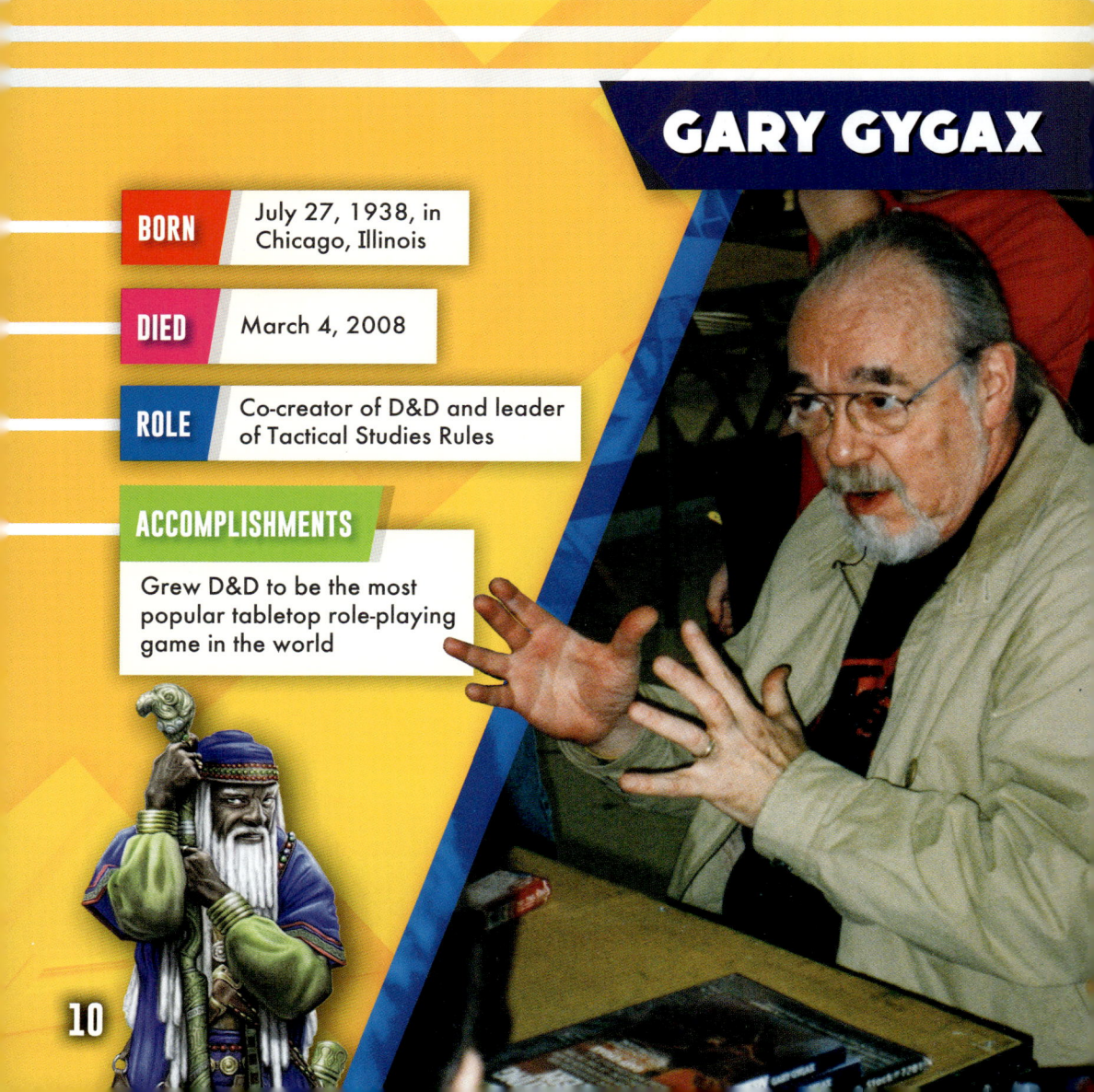

ORIGINAL D&D BOOKLETS

The original game contained three booklets. *Men & Magic* introduces the game's rules. Players learn about character **classes**, species, languages, and abilities. They also learn how to perform actions through dice rolls. *Monsters & Treasure* introduces the game's monsters and items that can be found. *The Underworld & Wilderness Adventures* introduces settings that players can explore.

BASEMENT BORN

Gary tried to sell the original version of D&D to other gaming companies. But no one would buy it. The booklets had to be handmade in Gary's basement!

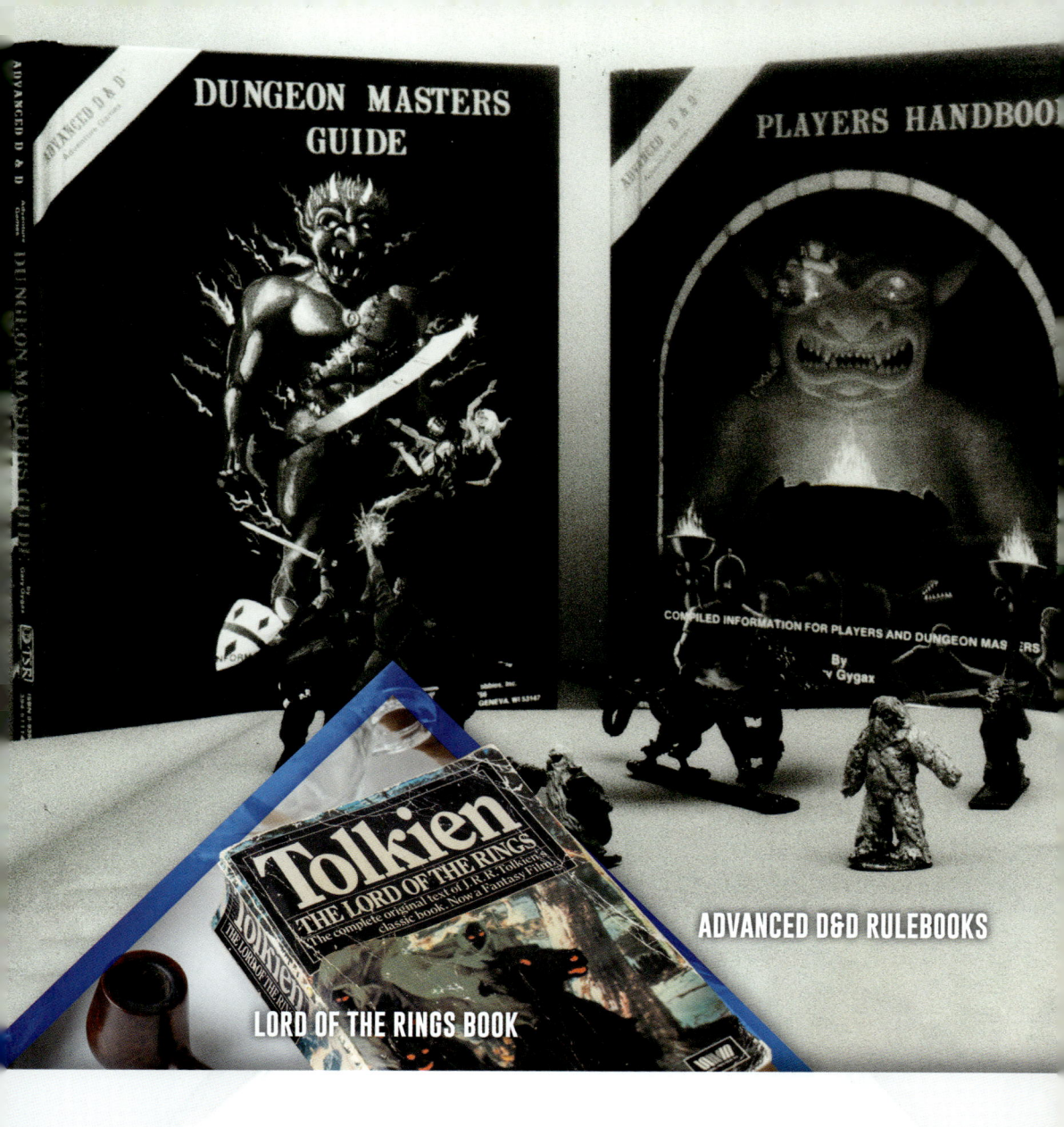

DUNGEON MASTERS GUIDE

PLAYERS HANDBOOK

COMPILED INFORMATION FOR PLAYERS AND DUNGEON MASTERS

By
Gary Gygax

ADVANCED D&D RULEBOOKS

LORD OF THE RINGS BOOK

Tolkien
THE LORD OF THE RINGS
The complete original text of J.R.R. Tolkien's
classic book. Now a Fantasy Film

The game changed and grew. In 1977, D&D divided into basic and advanced versions. Advanced D&D added three new rulebooks. *Monster Manual* listed every monster. *Players Handbook* expanded the game's rules. *Dungeon Masters Guide* provided information about running campaigns.

Another big change was the result of a **lawsuit**. D&D took inspiration from J.R.R. Tolkien's Lord of the Rings book series. D&D used similar creatures. TSR was forced to change some names in D&D. Hobbits became halflings. Balrogs became balor. These small changes helped avoid big costs!

COMMON D&D SPECIES

ELF
Life Span: around 750 years
Skills: Darkvision, advantage against being charmed

DWARF
Life Span: around 350 years
Skills: Darkvision, resistance to poison damage

TIEFLING
Life Span: around 100 years
Skills: Darkvision, resistance to fire damage

HUMAN
Life Span: around 100 years
Skill: ability score increase

HALFLING
Life Span: around 150 years
Skills: Lucky Reroll, advantage against being frightened

More problems arose in the 1980s. Some people were concerned that D&D promoted harmful activities. Some groups disagreed with the magic in the game. They also wondered if D&D promoted violence.

DUNGEONS & DRAGONS CARTOON

D&D TIMELINE

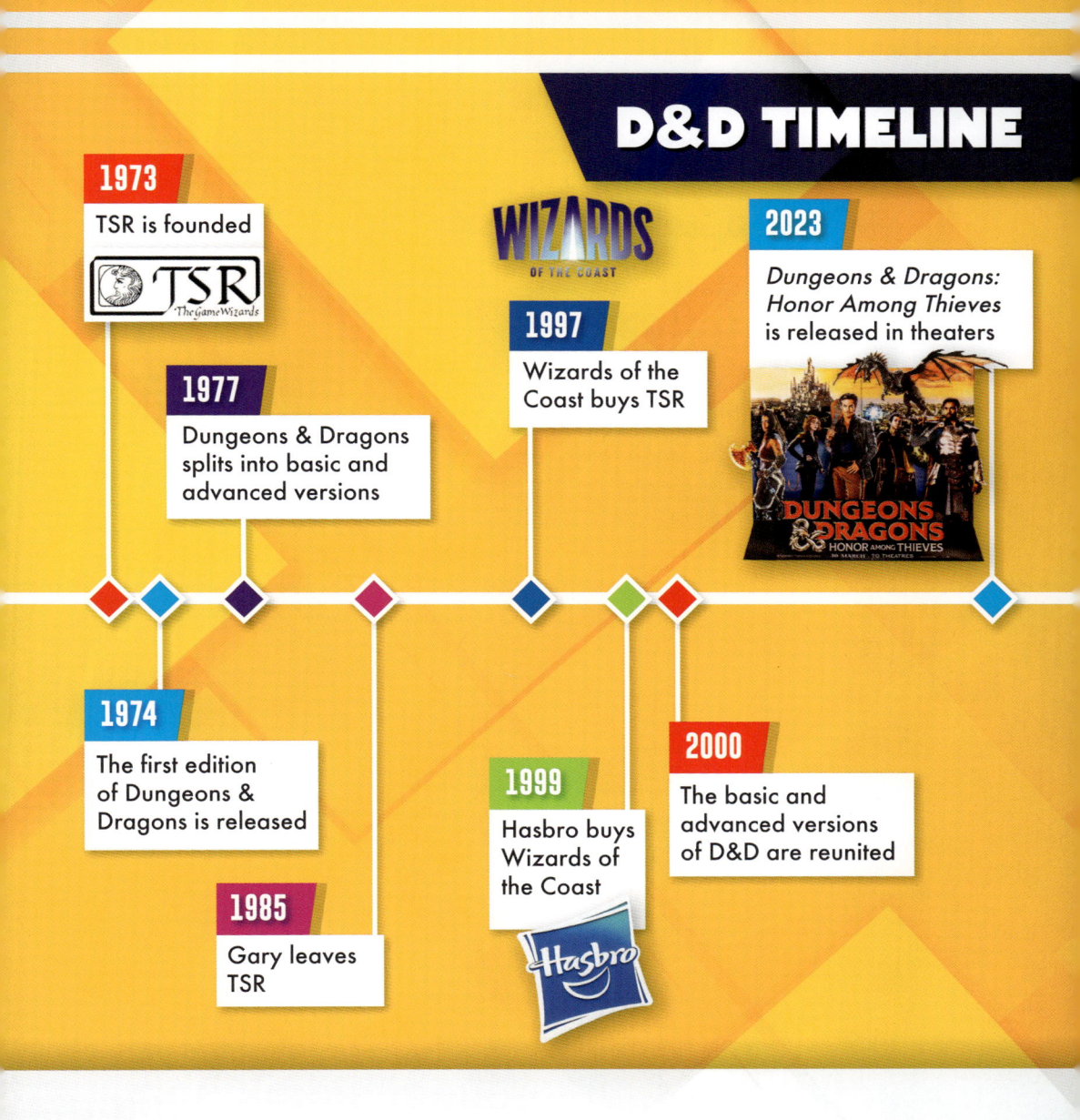

1973
TSR is founded

1977
Dungeons & Dragons splits into basic and advanced versions

1974
The first edition of Dungeons & Dragons is released

1985
Gary leaves TSR

WIZARDS
OF THE COAST

1997
Wizards of the Coast buys TSR

1999
Hasbro buys Wizards of the Coast

2000
The basic and advanced versions of D&D are reunited

2023
Dungeons & Dragons: Honor Among Thieves is released in theaters

Still, D&D was very popular. In 1982, the game was released in 22 countries outside the United States. It was translated into many different languages. More than 3 million people played the game. In 1983, a cartoon called *Dungeons & Dragons* first aired. It was popular, though many people thought it was too violent. It aired until 1985.

In 1987, TSR released the Forgotten Realms Campaign Set. It included two books describing a new world full of history, characters, and places to explore. It was very popular. Many D&D products are still based on it!

READ ALL ABOUT IT!

TSR wanted new ways to profit from D&D. The company decided to release books based on the game. The stories took place in popular D&D settings.

SECOND EDITION ADVANCED D&D BOOKS

1991 *SPELLJAMMER* BOX SET

The second edition of Advanced D&D was released in 1989. It included updated rulebooks and new information about the game. Some monsters from the game were removed or renamed. TSR also released **supplements** to the game. *Spelljammer* was released in 1989. This supplement included an outer space setting!

17

NEW ENCOUNTERS

HASBRO HEADQUARTERS

By the 1990s, TSR was not making enough money. People worried it would not last. Some fans were unhappy with how TSR was shaping D&D. In 1997, Wizards of the Coast bought TSR. Many fans were happy with this change. They hoped WotC would make the game better. In 1999, WotC became a part of the toy company Hasbro.

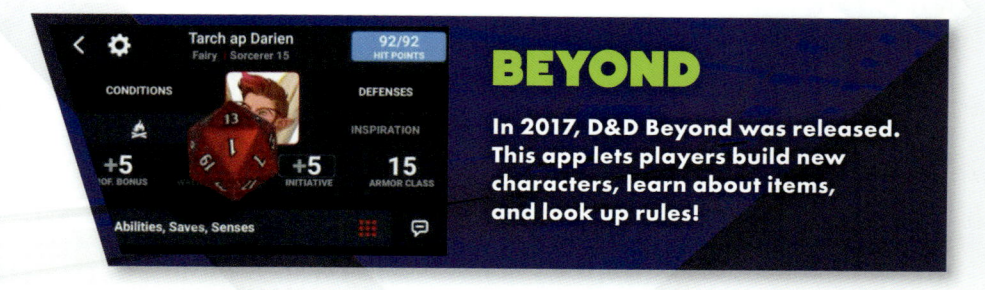

BEYOND

In 2017, D&D Beyond was released. This app lets players build new characters, learn about items, and look up rules!

In 2000, the third edition of D&D was released. It brought the basic and advanced versions of D&D back together. In 2008, the fourth edition of D&D came out. New rules about magic were added.

D&D EDITIONS

1974	**FIRST EDITION**
1989	**SECOND EDITION**
2000	**THIRD EDITION**
2008	**FOURTH EDITION**
2014	**FIFTH EDITION**
2024	**D&D 2024**

D&D's fifth edition was released in 2014. New rules changed how characters gain power and how players roll in different situations. In time, many new game books for the fifth edition were released. The popularity of the fifth edition grew in 2020. The COVID-19 **pandemic** caused people to stay home. Some began playing D&D online. Sales grew drastically.

DIE TYPES

D20

Common Uses: attacks, skill checks, ability checks, saving throws

D12

Common Use: damage from large weapons

D10

Common Use: two dice used to roll for percentages

D8

Common Use: damage from large weapons

D6

Common Use: character creation

D4

Common Uses: healing spells or damage from small weapons

In 2024, WotC released D&D 2024. This new edition updated the rules and added new character classes. New rulebooks added spells and made changes to how players could fight. It also included different settings.

FUTURE PLANS

WotC and Starbreeze Entertainment have partnered to make an online multiplayer game based on D&D. The project will get an official name when it launches sometime in 2026.

ICEWIND DALE

Beyond the game, fans enjoy many activities. Some listen to D&D **podcasts** to get news and learn to play. Others play video games. Many enjoyed 2000's *Icewind Dale* and 2015's *Sword Coast Legends*.

EARLY GAME

In 1981, *Dungeons & Dragons Computer Fantasy Game* was released. This handheld game sold out quickly!

There have been D&D movies, too. In 2000, the movie *Dungeons & Dragons* was released. Many did not like the movie's story or **special effects**. In 2023, the movie *Dungeons & Dragons: Honor Among Thieves* was released. More people enjoyed this movie. It made over $208 million worldwide!

2000 *DUNGEONS & DRAGONS* MOVIE

DUNGEONS & DRAGONS: HONOR AMONG THIEVES

DUNGEONS & DONATIONS

WotC gives back to the community. Every year, the company hosts the Extra Life **fundraiser** for Children's Miracle Network hospitals. They raise money by streaming D&D campaigns and selling special items. In 2020, they raised $520,000! WotC also supports the Trevor Project. In 2022, WotC **donated** over $1.3 million to the organization. A special dice set was released in 2024. Sales supported the Trevor Project!

WotC gives game kits to schools and libraries, too. In 2023, the company gave 200 D&D kits to classrooms across the United States. In 2024, the company gave 75 kits to Washington libraries.

GIVING BACK

$520,000
RAISED FOR CHILDREN'S MIRACLE NETWORK HOSPITALS IN 2020

OVER **$1.3 MILLION** GIVEN TO THE TREVOR PROJECT IN 2022

200 D&D KITS GIVEN TO CLASSROOMS IN 2023

75 D&D KITS GIVEN TO WASHINGTON LIBRARIES IN 2024

FAN-MADE FUN

COSPLAYING

PAINTED FIGURINE

Fans celebrate D&D together. Many enjoy creative activities such as **cosplaying** their characters. Others like to paint figurines and make special dice for players to use in their games. **Homebrewing** is also common. DMs create their own stories and rules for campaigns.

A LONG CAMPAIGN

The longest-running game of D&D has been going on for over 40 years! Over time, more than 50 people have been part of the game.

Events also get fans together. D&D Direct gives fans a look at what is coming to the game. The 2024 D&D Direct was live-streamed online. It gave information about a new D&D-themed LEGO set. A D&D-themed *Magic: The Gathering* card set was also announced.

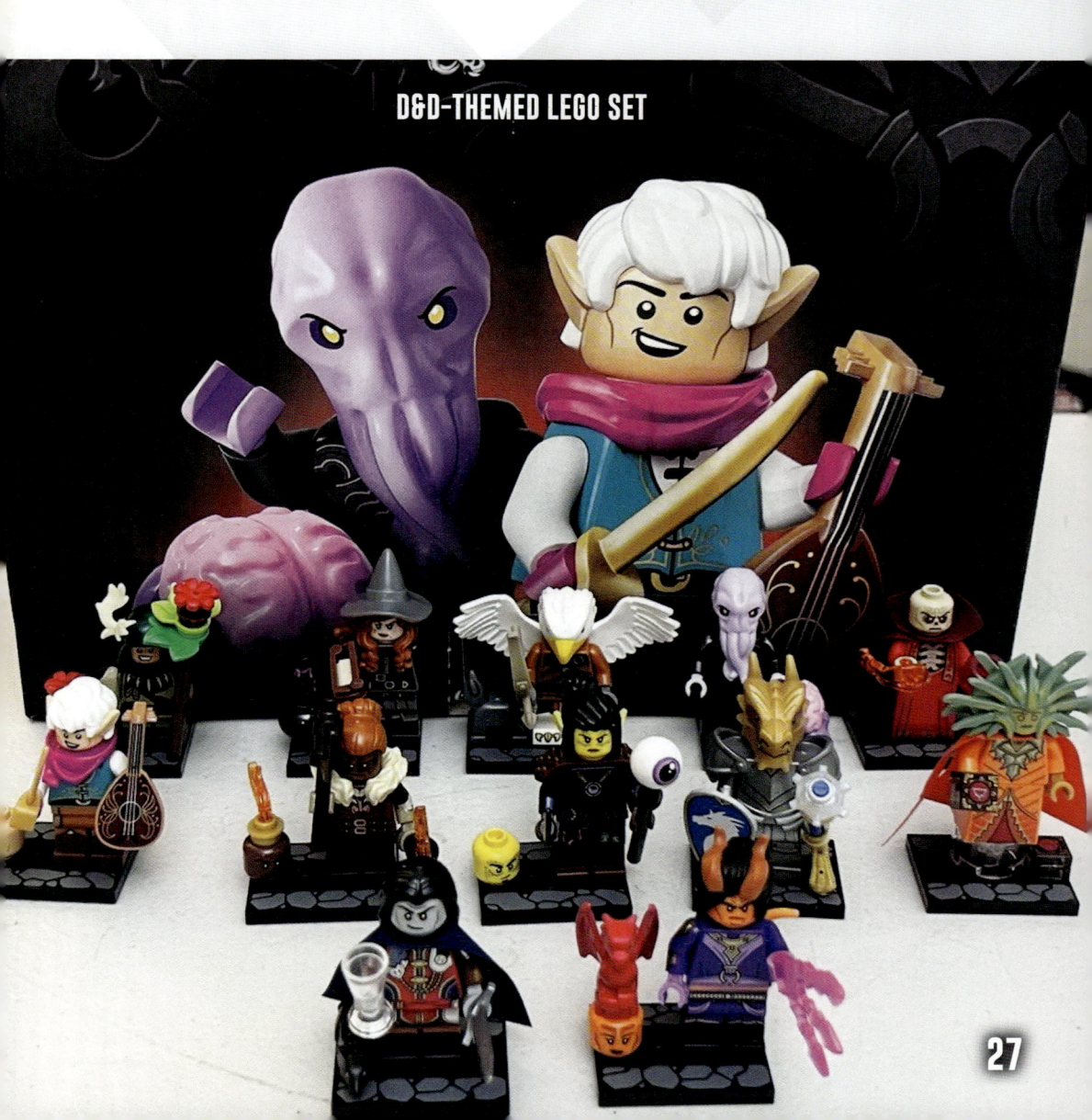

D&D-THEMED LEGO SET

GEN CON

GARY CON

Conventions also attract D&D fans. Gary Con is held in Lake Geneva, Wisconsin, each year. In 2024, over 3,000 fans gathered to learn about D&D, play games together, and more!

Gen Con is even more popular. Thousands of tabletop gaming fans gather in Indiana. They play board games and role-playing games such as D&D. In 2024, visitors could buy an advance copy of the newest edition of the *Player's Handbook*. Many enjoy the creativity that D&D brings. The game helps people make friends and build community!

GEN CON

WHAT IT IS
A tabletop gaming convention first created by Gary Gygax

FIRST HELD
1968 in Lake Geneva, Wisconsin

WHEN IT HAPPENS
Once every year

WHERE IT HAPPENS
Indianapolis, Indiana

PEOPLE IN ATTENDANCE
More than 71,000 in 2024

GLOSSARY

apps—programs such as games or internet browsers; apps are also called applications.

campaign—an ongoing story led by a dungeon master

classes—character roles that determine a character's strengths and abilities

conventions—events where fans of a subject meet

cosplaying—dressing up as a character from a movie, book or video game

donated—gave money or other things to people in need

dungeon master—a person who runs a D&D campaign by creating the story, setting up challenges, and directing the game

fundraiser—an event where money is raised for a specific cause

headquarters—a company's main office

homebrewing—playing using content that is not in a rulebook

lawsuit—a disagreement brought before a court

medieval—related to a period of time from the year 500 to the year 1500 that is known as the Middle Ages

pandemic—an outbreak of a disease that happens over a wide area and affects many people

podcasts—programs people can listen to on the internet

role-playing game—a game in which players take on the roles of characters to complete the game

special effects—effects that use makeup, special props, camera systems, computer graphics, and other methods to make fake things look real

strategies—plans of action to achieve a goal

supplements—materials added to something to change it or make it better

wargames—games in which players roleplay the different sides of an armed conflict

TO LEARN MORE

AT THE LIBRARY

Braun, Eric. *J. R. R. Tolkien: Epic Fantasy Author.* Minneapolis, Minn.: Lerner Publications, 2022.

Hicks, Gabe. *A Kid's Guide to Tabletop RPGs: Exploring Dice, Game Systems, Roleplaying, and More.* Philadelphia, Pa.: Running Press, 2023.

Rae, Susie. *Inside the World of Dungeons & Dragons.* New York, N.Y.: Harper Collins, 2022.

ON THE WEB

FACTSURFER

Factsurfer.com gives you a safe, fun way to find more information.

1. Go to www.factsurfer.com.

2. Enter "Dungeons & Dragons" into the search box and click Q.

3. Select your book cover to see a list of related content.

INDEX